Immortal moments of bravery,
destruction and death relived in the great
photographs of the war, and in
brilliant eyewitness descriptions by
outstanding writers and
reporters including Winston Churchill,
John Dos Passos, Ernest
Hemingway and dozens of others.

THE GREAT WAR

The famous battles—the Marne, Caporetto,
Verdun, the Somme, Ypres,
Belleau Wood—gas attacks, civilian panic,
dogfights over the trenches, tank
s through fields of
ayonet fighting,
l experience of the
s and pictures.

THE YANKS
ARE COMING

PIERCE G. FREDERICKS

BANTAM  BOOKS

BANTAM PATHFINDER EDITIONS

NEW YORK / TORONTO / LONDON

RLI: $\dfrac{\text{VLM } 9.0}{\text{IL } 8.12}$

A Bantam Book / published November 1964
Bantam Pathfinder edition published April 1966

Library of Congress Catalog Card Number: 64-7657

Cover painting courtesy THE MARINE CORPS GAZETTE
by Tom Lovell.

Published simultaneously in the United States and Canada

Bantam Books are published by Bantam Books, Inc., a subsidiary
of Grosset & Dunlap, Inc. Its trade-mark, consisting of the words
"Bantam Books" and the portrayal of a bantam, is registered in the
United States Patent Office and in other countries. Marca Registrada.
Bantam Books, Inc., 271 Madison Avenue, New York, N. Y. 10016.

PRINTED IN THE UNITED STATES OF AMERICA

EUROPE ON THE EVE OF WORLD WAR I

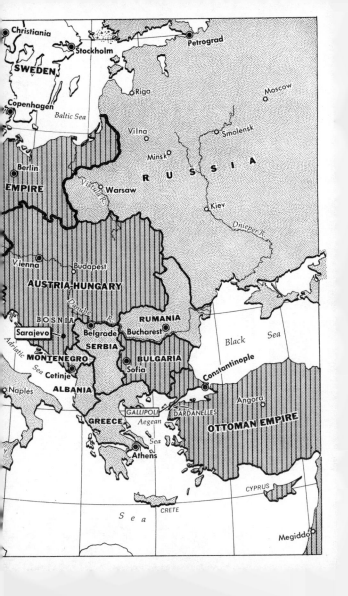

To Begin with . . .

1

3

5

2

6

8

The world was at peace. Three of the most powerful European thrones were occupied by first cousins: George V of England (5), Nicholas II of Russia (4) and Wilhelm II of Germany (2). But nationalistic feelings were a dominant force in every European country, large and small; the major powers had seized colonial empires that girdled the globe—with England acquiring the lion's share; and military expenditures were at an all-time high. The bitter rivalries which lay beneath the surface of imperial accord made it possible for the murder of one man to precipitate a war in which ten million men would die. Franz Ferdinand (6), heir to the throne of Austria, was assassinated in the Austro-Hungarian subject state of Bosnia by a Bosnian student named Gavrilo Princip (1). This would appear to make it a Bosnian matter, but the victim's uncle, Emperor Franz Josef (3), deeply desired an excuse to go to war with Bosnia's neighbor, Serbia. He feared that Serbia was about to form a coalition of Balkan states and lead it against his doddering Empire. Accordingly it suited him to believe that the plot had actually been hatched in Serbia's capital, Belgrade. An attack on Serbia, though, was likely to mean that Austria-Hungary would in turn be attacked by Russia, big brother of all small Slavic states. Austria-Hungary's ally Germany had to be consulted: Would she deal with Russia while the Austro-Hungarians dealt with Serbia? Before he could answer the question, the Kaiser had to consider that Russia and France had an alliance. If he went to war with one, he went to war with both. Thus, the buck stops in Berlin on the desk of the Kaiser, a man of much military bombast, a withered arm and the nagging notion that Germany was somehow being denied her rightful "place in the sun." He could have had the domination of Europe without a war —both his industry and his intelligent, hard-working people were increasing faster than anyone else's. His nation was as safe as one reasonably can be—it had the finest army in the world and a navy nearly as good as the British. Yet Wilhelm voted for war. Why? It helps to remember that Germany was the last nation in Europe to be united. Wilhelm had talked tough and won national approval; when the crisis came, he was heavily committed and lacked the courage to back down. The assassin (right) at Sarajevo had fired his shots on June 28. In the slow way of old-time diplomacy it would take a month for the shooting war to start.

10

Call
to
Arms

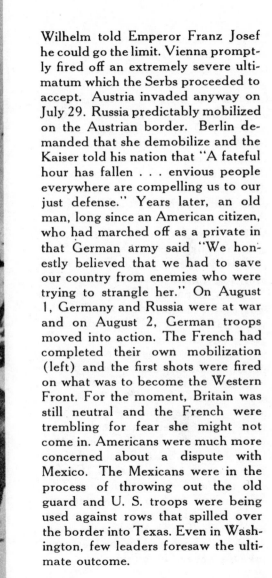

Wilhelm told Emperor Franz Josef he could go the limit. Vienna promptly fired off an extremely severe ultimatum which the Serbs proceeded to accept. Austria invaded anyway on July 29. Russia predictably mobilized on the Austrian border. Berlin demanded that she demobilize and the Kaiser told his nation that "A fateful hour has fallen . . . envious people everywhere are compelling us to our just defense." Years later, an old man, long since an American citizen, who had marched off as a private in that German army said "We honestly believed that we had to save our country from enemies who were trying to strangle her." On August 1, Germany and Russia were at war and on August 2, German troops moved into action. The French had completed their own mobilization (left) and the first shots were fired on what was to become the Western Front. For the moment, Britain was still neutral and the French were trembling for fear she might not come in. Americans were much more concerned about a dispute with Mexico. The Mexicans were in the process of throwing out the old guard and U. S. troops were being used against rows that spilled over the border into Texas. Even in Washington, few leaders foresaw the ultimate outcome.

German Foreign Minister Theobald von Bethmann-Hollweg sent his troops (right) off with the cry "Let your hearts beat for God and your fists on the enemy." Then he sent an ultimatum to Belgium, whose neutrality Germany had guaranteed by treaty. The demand was that German troops be allowed to pass through unimpeded. Belgium replied that she could not, with honor, accept and resisted the invasion. Britain, until now on the side lines and hoping for peace, was also a guarantor of Belgium neutrality. She protested to Berlin and Bethmann-Hollweg called the Belgium treaty "a scrap of paper." Britain went to war and Foreign Secretary Sir Edward Grey noted "The lights are going out all over Europe. We shall not see them lit again in our lifetime." A British liner which was to become famous—the Lusitania—slipped out of New York harbor to avoid German battleships which were said (falsely) to be lying in wait. German troops hurrying to the front on their marvelously efficient railroad system waved signs "Excursion to Paris" from their cars. The "Excursion" had to be via Belgium and it would have a very heavy effect on the war. The French had the good sense to lie back and let the Germans take the onus of invading.

Though invasion of Belgium meant
that Britain was pulled into the war,
it was nevertheless inevitable because it was part of "The Plan."
"The Plan" was the masterpiece
of Count Alfred von Schlieffen
(above), former chief of the German General Staff. It called for the
main German thrust to get around
the French flank by sweeping across
Belgium, then rolling up the enemy
line. Only minimum forces were to
be left to hold the expected French
attacks at the other end of the front.
The watchword was "Keep the right
wing strong!" And strong it was.
One Englishman fighting near Mons
told a reporter afterward:

The Germans (above) came up like a crowd leaving Hampstead Park. They came marching up in droves, firing their rifles from their right hips. They have absolutely no idea of aim. But if their rifle work was bad, there is no doubt about their accuracy with the machine gun.

A little girl near the battle wrote:

We went to bed at 9:30 last night, but could not sleep as the floor was hard and cold and the noise was awful. At 3:30 A.M., we went to Mass and then back to bed again. La Mère told us to pray a great deal as we might die at any moment.

The tiny, ill-trained Belgian army (left) made one stand in the fortresses around Liége and then was swept back. The British, under General Sir John French, a leader of the most modest talents, held at Mons until their steady, quick-firing infantrymen were outflanked. At Le Cateau they made a second stand, were pushed out and lost a part of their artillery when it was knocked out covering the retreat. The French right, attacking farther south, was making little progress and taking heavy losses against machine guns. In the center, the Germans were thrusting the French back and marching ahead day after day in spite of the fearful August heat. A gallant French attack at Guise slowed them briefly, then they came on again, ever closer to Paris. An infantryman wrote of it:

We were in the trenches waiting for them, but we didn't expect anything like the mashing blow that struck us. All at once . . . the sky began to rain down bullets and shells. At first the shells went very wide, for their fire was bad, but after a time —I think it was a long time—they got our range and then they fairly mopped us up. I saw shells bursting to the right and left of me and I saw many a good comrade go out.

21

French Commander-in-Chief Joseph
Joffre (above) was a patient and
stolid man—and, for the moment,
very lucky to be so. His attacks
(right) against the German lines
were coming to nothing. The im-
perturbable waited for a chance to
counter. The chance was coming.
The Russians had opened strongly
pushing into East Prussia. Germany
sent four divisions from the Western Front to help out. "Keep the
right wing strong," Schlieffen had
said. It had started weaker than he
had wished; more divisions had
been detached to police Belgium
and now four more were gone. Then
another heresy was committed. Instead of swinging the right flank west
of Paris, German General Alexander
von Kluck pulled it in to pass east
of the French capital and the chance
Joffre awaited was now at hand.

As the weakened German right swept past Paris it lacked enough divisions to cover its flank properly. General Joseph Gallieni, commander of the Paris garrison, begged Joffre to let him strike. Joffre finally agreed and asked that the British (above) also attack, but British General Sir John French expected no victory. Joffre urged him vigorously:

Carried away by my convictions and the gravity of the moment, I remember bringing down my fist on a table and crying "Monsieur le Marechal, the honor of England is at stake!"

General French agreed and if the British advance was less than rapid, the net result of the Allied attack beginning on September 5 was to push the Germans far back over the Marne. A German soldier wrote:

The enemy's artillery mowed the ground with its fire. In one minute's time, I counted 40 shells. The shrapnel exploded nearer and nearer; at last it reached our ranks . . . the shrieks of the wounded rang out on all sides. Tears came to my eyes when I heard the poor devils moaning with pain (see following page).

The German dream of ending the war in one swift campaign had failed. Now both sides began a race to occupy the empty ground which lay between the Marne battlefield and the English Channel. When they finished, there was a true "front" all across France. Sir John French (above) and his battered English regulars (right) went to the Channel end of the line near the Belgian city of Ypres—"Wipers" to the Tommies. They found themselves on October 20 facing a new German offensive manned largely by volunteers aflame with patriotism. Ardent young Germans threw themselves against the dogged defense the British do so well. The old professionals were making a last stand. When the battles were over they would have taken 50,000 casualties and the Regular Army would be no more.

The German troops that mauled the British positions around Ypres had a manpower edge of better than two to one. As attack after attack came down the axis of the road from Menin, a little town east of Ypres, it seemed that they must break through. Sir John French wrote:

October 31st and November 1st will remain for ever memorable in the history of our country, for, during these two days, no more than one thin and straggling line of tired-out British soldiers stood between the Empire and its practical ruin as an independent first-class Power . . . Right, center, and left our men were tried and pressed as troops were never tried and pressed before.

The Germans did not get through. What they had called "A contemptible little army" held them, plugging the holes they made from a scanty reserve which sometimes included cooks and company clerks. By mid-November, cold weather and exhaustion closed down the Western Front for 1914 and the trench lines (left) ran from Switzerland to the English Channel. They were not yet the elaborate trench systems with their underground dugouts in which men would live for weeks at a time.

31

As the war at sea opened, the British enjoyed an edge of twenty to thirteen over the Germans in modern battleships. The edge was as good or better in most other classes of ships including, surprisingly, 65 submarines against approximately 28 for the Germans. The British also had an aggressive First Lord of the Admiralty named Winston Churchill who did good service in late September by landing a brigade of Royal Marines at Ostend to create a distraction on the Channel coast until the army could take over from them. A second early fray went badly for the English when two German cruisers eluded their forces in the Mediterranean and holed up in Turkey. Still, it was felt that the German Fleet was no match for its adversary, and in 1914, very few people foresaw the work an untested weapon that Germans called the U-boat (right) would do. True, one sub sank three old British cruisers, but it was 1915, before the realization began to grow that German submarines might be able to blockade England just as effectively as English surface ships could blockade Germany. The U-boat would grow into the greatest threat to British naval supremacy since Trafalgar. By 1917, the submarines would nearly starve Britain out.

On the Eastern Front, the war began with Austria invading Serbia as befits a large power intent on chastising a smaller one. In equipment, the Austrians had the better of it since the Serbs made do with such primitive devices as ox-drawn artillery (right). To the dismay of Vienna, the unrepentant Serbs sent the first Austrian push reeling back. A second attempt in September met the same fate in fighting of Hatfield-McCoy savagery. In November, the Austrians tried again and this time it seemed that the chastisement might work, until the Serbs put in a last-ditch counterattack which sent the Austrians back to their own frontier. An observer wrote:

Outside the mud was a foot deep and the rain coming down in a steady, drenching downpour. The wounded began to arrive around six, in the cold light of dawn. The air was frightful. The men had been on the road for a week . . . with nothing but their first aid dressings.

Nor were things going better on the Russian front. The Czar's armies had mobilized a good deal more quickly than anyone imagined they could. Now they were pushing the Austrians back and threatening the German ally on the northern flank.

[**War in the East**]

If the German had contempt for the French he had hatred for the Russian. Hans Hanssen, a Reichstag member, reported a Berlin scene:

Spirits are not so jubilant in Berlin as they were a week ago. Reports from the battlefields are not so stimulating to the nerves. The High Command has already pampered the morale of those at home. At least one victory a day is demanded. When that fails, general apathy is evident. The war spirit is passing into the background because of the desire for amusement. One sees many women dressed in black and many unemployed. A poor, undernourished suffering family . . . was standing on Potsdamer Platz, selling homemade wooden swords at ten pfennigs apiece. The swords were painted green, and written on each of them in large red letters were these words: "Each shot—a Russian." Brutality is on the increase.

The Russians (right) had actually been on the soil of Prussia. Moving up with a heavy advantage in numbers, they had forced back the German army before them. The German High Command quickly exhumed a retired general named Paul von Hindenburg and rushed him to the shaky Eastern front.

Two Russian armies were advancing with the Masurian Lakes between them and no co-ordination. Working from plans drawn by Colonel Max Hoffmann the Germans left a screen in front of the northern army and rushed south to crush the Russians in the battle of Tannenberg (below). A German regimental historian saw them this way:

With morning gray a long enemy column of all arms came slowly out of the woods without any protecting troops and offered a target which would never have been permitted at peace maneuvers. Unfortunately,

fire was opened on it too soon by some excited riflemen; upon which the general fire of both battalions and the machine gun company was opened . . . more fearful effect can hardly be imagined. The Russians tried to take refuge in the woods, abandoning vehicles and horses . . . but very soon they exhibited white cloths on poles and rifles.

A British observer said simply:

The Russians were just great big-hearted children who had thought out nothing and had stumbled half asleep into a wasp's nest.

The New Technology of Warfare

As 1915 dawned, the trench lines were drawn across France and the machine gun, which was going to characterize the remainder of the war, was coming into its own. It was not a new weapon. As early as 1857, a Belgian had a device with 50 barrels which could fire about 100 shots a minute, and by 1884, an American named Hiram Maxim had developed a fully automatic gun. The Germans (above) were so impressed that they had some 50,000 of them on hand when the war opened. Authorities have estimated that the machine gun inflicted 80 percent of all casualties.

The first attempt to find an answer to the machine gun was to enormously increase the amount of artillery (left) used with an attack. All the major combatants had gone into the war with about the same equipment. The light or field gun was approximately a three-incher. The famous French 75 was one of these. The heavy artillery began at six inches and grew steadily larger. In 1915, the first attempts were made to shield the infantry. An attack was preceded by a heavy artillery bombardment which was continued after the infantry moved out (the range being lengthened as the troops advanced). Soon generals were calling for heavier bombardments until by 1917, two or three million rounds were being used before a major attack. The tactic was self-defeating. The bombardments lasted so long that any chance of surprise was lost, and the ground became so ferociously churned up that ammunition and supplies could not be moved forward rapidly to support a breakthrough even if one was achieved. Once the enemy learned that attacks began with heavy bombardments, they simply built deeper dugouts to which they retired until the opposing gunners had to lift fire for fear of hitting their own troops.

As spring came in 1915, it was the French intention to attack ferociously in about the same mass formations that had cost them so many casualties the year before (right). They had yet to learn that élan is no match for machine guns. The British hoped merely to hold on until Commonwealth divisions and the new army being raised in England could arrive to replace the Expeditionary Force which had died at Ypres. The Germans planned to hold the Western Front lightly and send their weight east to destroy the Russians. They did, however, have a new weapon they wanted to try; the attempt was made at Ypres on April 22. A mixed bag of Allied troops was holding the line. A Canadian describes the action:

As on the two preceding days, a motley crowd of refugees was shuffling along the road from Ypres to Poperinghe. In scattered groups they went, in Sunday black or rags: old men sweating between the shafts of handcarts piled high with household treasures; deep chested dogs harnessed underneath and straining at the axle with lolling tongue; aged women on wagons stacked with bedding or trundled in wheel barrows. . . . the evening brought the new weapon of attack (following page).

Soon after four o'clock in the afternoon, the German guns shorted their range to begin a violent bombardment. General Alderson could see two clouds of yellowish green. These drifted slowly southwards, close to the ground and spread laterally until they united in one long low rolling bank of choking horrible fog. Stumbling and gasping in an agony of terror-stricken flight before it, scattered groups of French African infantrymen with reeking yellowed clothing and ashen purple faces, staggered across the fields . . . regardless of everything but this unknown devil which had them by the throat . . . The cloud moved before the gentle breeze at the rate of five or six miles an hour. . . At three miles from the cylinders the density was still great enough to hurt the eyes, make noses run and to make men vomit violently. . . . There came stragglers from the 87th struggling for breath with sobs of "Pauvre France!"

Poison gas—chlorine—had been used for the first time in war. Stout-fighting Canadians with damp handkerchiefs over their mouths plugged the hole and soon gas masks (right) arrived to prevent gas from becoming a weapon that could change the course of the war.

50

When the war had begun, the Americans were almost unanimously in favor of remaining neutral. President Woodrow Wilson had declared "Every man who really loves America will act and speak in the true spirit of neutrality." The British blockade of Germany brought some loss of trade, but Allied military orders more than made up the difference and the economy swirled up in a boomlet. Then on May 1, 1915, the English liner Lusitania set sail from New York with 2000 passengers aboard. The same day the Imperial German Embassy had put

an ad in several newspapers reminding Americans that those who sailed in British ships did so at their own risk. On May 7, the submarine U-20 caught the Lusitania off southern Ireland and put a torpedo into her starboard side. She sank in 15 minutes, and over half her passengers died— 124 of them Americans. A shocked Woodrow Wilson fired a note off to Berlin demanding that submarines not be used against merchant ships. Berlin sent an evasive reply. The issue that would bring America into the war had arisen.

A French offensive in May ground to a halt with over 100,000 casualties, but by September Joffre was ready to try again. The main French attack was to come in the white-chalk country east of Reims; a smaller French-British attack was to go in around Loos. Near Reims, the first thrusts got through only to run into defenses in depth and stagger back, exhausted (right) with small gains and casualties almost double those of the Germans. Nor was the blood-letting all one sided. The British reporter Sir Philip Gibbs saw a group of German prisoners:

. . . sleeping, in huddled grotesque postures, like dead men. Others were awake, sitting hunched up, with drooping head and a beaten, exhausted look . . . Many of them were dying and a German ambulance man went among them injecting them with morphine to ease the agony which made them writhe and groan . . . A friend of mine carried a water jar to some of the wounded and held it to their lips. One of them refused. He was a tall, evil looking fellow with a bloody rag around his head—a typical "Hun," I thought. But he pointed to a comrade who lay gasping beside him and said, in German, "He needs it first."

Neither Sir John French nor his First Army commander, Sir Douglas Haig, had been enthusiastic about the attack. They had seasoned troops to lead with (left) but nothing except green divisions for the follow-up. They got off well—one soldier of the London Irish kicked a football off the parapet and dribbled it all the way to the German lines—but then the front bogged down. Sir Philip Gibbs described it:

While the Highlanders went forward with their pipes, two brigades of the Londoners, on their right, were advancing in the direction of the long double slag heap, southwest of Loos. . . . Some of them were blowing mouth organs, playing the music hall song of "Hullo, hullo, it's a different girl again" and the "Robert E. Lee" until one after another a musician fell in a crumpled heap . . . Again and again they crawled forward and up, but the blasts of machine gun fire mowed them down and many young Scots lay motionless on those chalky slopes with their kilts riddled with bullets. "Where are the supports?" asked the Scottish officers. "In God's name, where are the troops who were to follow on? Why did we do all this bloody fighting to be hung up out here like this?" (following page).

By the fall the French government was having its doubts about Joffre (center), but the Hero of the Marne remained. The English, however, had had quite enough of Sir John French. His successor was the commander of the British First Army, Sir Douglas Haig (left). Sir Douglas was on the record as not thinking much of his former boss:

I had grave doubts whether either his temper was sufficiently even or his military knowledge sufficiently thorough to enable him to be an effective commander.

In later years, there would be many whose grave doubts about Haig would make him the chief victim of a German statement that the British Army was composed of lions, but led by donkeys. Other writers are willing to concede that he may have been an old-time Empire builder with all the stubbornness of the breed, but he was staunch. When the line seemed about to break, he managed to hold it. And he could make up his mind—if sometimes with the most calamitous results. To make certain that Sir Douglas had the cannon, the shells and the machine guns to fight with, the British also appointed a new Minister of Munitions —David Lloyd George (right).

{ **Russian Debacle** }

The Russians, now under Grand Duke Nicholas, continued to fight right through the winter. Against the Austrians in the Carpathians, they had some success, but the Austrians had now been beefed up with German divisions (left) and as a Russian said:

Fighting the Germans is quite a different matter from fighting the Austrians. The German shell falls right into our trenches and there is an extraordinary amount of it.

In the north, a Ludendorff offensive rocked the Russians back, then went on to gain ground against troops who were running out of rifles and were very short on artillery. A British observer wrote:

In tactics the Gemans win against anything like equal numbers if the Russians have not time to entrench. The Russians have less idea of manoeuvre . . . (they) suffer from the lack of shell, of heavy artillery and of machine guns. It is believed that the Germans have four machine guns per battalion and they do not spare shell. I heard of a battery commander (Russian) today who was told that he would be court-martialed if he fired more than three rounds per gun per diem.

The German aim was nothing less than the destruction of the Russian armies (right). The main thrust came in the Gorlice-Tarnow area where a concentration from some 1500 guns fell upon the Russian Third Army. No defenses in depth had been prepared and there was little artillery. A Russian said that

. . . his division was in action between Rojan and Ostrov when drafts of 1800 infantry arrived and were distributed to support trenches to wait unarmed until casualties in the firing-line should make rifles available. The Germans turned the Russian right and, he had seen, standing helpless through want of shell, 1600 of these unarmed drafts "churned to gruel" by the enemy's guns. Back fell the Russians, another attack slanting down on them from East Prussia: It was rumored that Mitau and Lomja had been lost, but the Russains were quite happy. They said: "We will retire to the Urals and when we get there the enemy's pursuing army will have dwindled to a single German and a single Austrian; The Austrian will give himself up as a prisoner and we will kill the German."

In all they retreated 300 miles and lost 750,000 men (following page).

The End Run That Failed

Then, in 1915, the Turks marched against Russia. A plea went to London for action against the Turks. London thought a naval demonstration against the Dardanelles straits might help. Winston Churchill saw a chance for something more—a long end run with British troops swarming through Turkey and eventually, perhaps, breaking the deadlock on the distant Western Front. Churchill had no great opinion of the generals:

They were altogether lacking that Supreme combination of the King-Warrior-Statesman . . . they were prevailingly of the heavy blockhead type . . . nerves much stronger than their imaginations.

For the moment no one was buying Churchill. In March a naval force went into the straits, had some ships sunk by mines, then turned around and went home. In April they were back, but by now the Turks (left) were ready for the landings at Gallipoli. A trooper relates:

The shrapnel fire became too warm to be pleasant and I said "Major, a soldier's first duty is to save his life for his country." He said "I quite agree, but must admit I don't see how it's to be done."

From April until the end of the year,
the outnumbered invaders (above)
tried to move up from their pre-
carious toeholds on the peninsula,
but the thing was not to be in spite
of the occasional capture of Turkish
patrols (right) and a great deal of
individual gallantry. British correspondent Henry Nevinson relates:

The captain twice led his company up against the Turkish trenches on Scimitar Hill, and twice was driven back. Collecting the men in a little hollow of the ground, he said "Now I depend on you, my lads, and we'll just have one more charge for the honor of the regiment." He led them all by a clear 20 yards up the hill, leapt into the trench, and there died.

A bitter winter came on, men were falling from disease and there was nothing for it but to evacuate:

The last day came ... At sunset, the guns fired their parting salute and were withdrawn ... A small party was left to keep up rifle-fire in the front trenches ... shortly before midnight the front line came in leaving lighted candles which at irregular intervals burned a string to discharge a rifle, so that a desultory fusillade was maintained for about an hour ... A party of 200 was to hold the fourth line to the last, and sacrifice themselves if the Turks attacked.

The withdrawal was brilliantly executed; but the campaign had been extremely costly: there were 250,-000 Allied casualties, and heavy losses of matériel, including several British warships (right).

Death
on the
Peaks

Both sides had been bidding eagerly for allies and they both offered the same rewards: pieces of other people's territory to be delivered after the victory. In May, the Entente made a sale—Italy came into the war against Austria, but not against Germany. Unfortunately for the new belligerent, the Italian-Austrian frontier is rugged alpine country (left). The Italians selected the least rugged area near the Isonzo River, made four drives (following page), lost a quarter of a million men before the year was out and got nowhere. The Central Powers did better with their new chum Bulgaria who attacked Serbia from the east. The Serbs made a fighting winter retreat to the Adriatic. A young lieutenant described it:

We threw ourselves into the water . . . The little ones fell and were carried away by the current . . . One of my old soldiers who was always beside me stopped. His clothes were white with ice. His face was distorted by the tremendous bitterness of an awful moment. He stared into the dim heavens, he spread out his red, cracked and bloody hands, shaking his fist toward the sky, and from his breast came a bitter vehement exclamation "God! God! Thou art not God!"

Fledglings and Aces

When the war began, it was only 13 years since the Wright brothers had flown the first airplane. Military aviation—what there was of it—was used only for observation (left). The infantry was so unfamiliar with the new gadget that it tended at first to fire on it at sight. A British Wing Commander said of the arrival of the first British troops:

We were rather sorry they had come, because up till that moment we had only been fired on by the French whenever we flew. Now we were fired on by French and British.

Insignia were put on the planes, crude bombing experiments were made by pilots who put a few hand grenades in their pockets, and in two-seater aircraft observers sometimes tried to shoot down opposing planes with rifles. In early 1915 the French introduced a crude device for firing a machine gun through a plane's propeller. Shortly thereafter a Dutch civilian named Anthony Fokker designed the first truly synchronized machine gun—it fired only when the propeller blade was not in line with it—and the true war in the air began. The planes of the day were rickety affairs whose top-level speed was approximately 70 miles an hour.

Before the machine gun, a British observer described the situation:

The first time I ever encountered a German machine in the air, both the pilot and myself were completely unarmed. Our machine had not been climbing well. As I was considered somewhat heavy for an observer (the pilot) told me to leave behind all unnecessary gear. We were taking photographs of the trench system to the north of Neuve Chapelle when I suddenly espied a German two-seater about 100 yards away and just below us . . . We waved a hand to the enemy and proceeded with our task. The enemy did likewise. At the time this did not appear to me in any way ridiculous—there is a bond of sympathy between all those who fly.

As the planes became better the hot-pursuit pilots, the aces, began to appear. For the Germans there was Max Immelmann "The Eagle of Lille" who perfected the Immelmann turn, the steady Oswald Boelcke (top left) and the Red Baron Manfred von Richthofen (top right). For the French there was the cold-blooded René Fonck (below left) and for the English a host of fine young airmen under General Sir Hugh Trenchard (below right).

For the moment, though, bombing was still a sideshow and eyes were on the knights of the air who went over the lines to engage in "dog fights" (right). The following is from the log of Edward Mannock:

Went over to Petit Vimy and Thelus in a sidecar this morning in an endeavour to pick up some relics of the last victims, down yesterday afternoon in flames. Regret that nothing remained of the machine. I met this unfortunate DFW at about 10,000 over Avion coming southwest, and I was traveling southeast. I could recognize the black crosses readily, (he was about 300 yards away and about 500 feet above me) so I turned my tail toward him and went in the same direction, thinking that if he were British he wouldn't take any notice of me and if a Hun I felt sure he would put his nose down and have a shot (thinking I hadn't seen him). The ruse worked beautifully. His nose went (point at me) and I immediately whipped around, dived and zoomed up behind him before he could say "knife." He tried to turn, but he was much too slow for the Nieuport. I got in about 50 rounds in short bursts while on the turn and he went down in flames, dropping pieces of wing and tail.

Learning to fly the rickety crates of the day was almost as fearsome as combat. Ted Parsons, a young American who flew for France in the Lafayette Escadrille wrote:

Despite all rumors to the contrary, the motors weren't taken from discarded motorcycles . . . Being of such light construction, the plane had plenty of give in the air. Frequently, in making a tight bank, I have looked back and seen the tail whipping around after me, bent in a perfect arc . . . When the student was first learning to crow-hop up

and down a field, he'd take off, rise about ten or twenty feet and then bring the ship down almost flat, hardly peaking at all, by blipping the motor on and off . . . Soon we learned to push the nose down a bit, then level off for a landing, just as if we had come in from a long flight instead of twenty feet . . . that's all there was to fly, except of course the next step which was take two or three times the altitude we had taken on crow hops and instead of coming right down, go on around the field with flat turns and then come down as we'd been doing.

While no one on the Allied side was paying much attention to "Boom" Trenchard's notions about bombing, the Germans were attempting to bomb London as early as the end of 1914. The first tries were made with planes which didn't have enough range for the job so Zeppelins (above) took up the task. The first London raid in May cost seven lives. It was 1916 before the English had combined blackouts, antiaircraft batteries and pursuit planes to win the first Battle of Britain. Here is a German captain's report of a raid made on Hull, a town in England:

I first threw a few bombs near the city to attract the searchlights and batteries, thus leading them to disclose their exact positions . . . I sent the L 11 at full speed ahead and turned into the wind over the city. For twenty minutes without being molested the bombs were placed at my direction . . . From the first I saw whole structures toppling into ruins . . . and people running to and fro in the glare of the fires . . . Four wickedly strong searchlights greeted us over the forts, but they could not spot us so were of no service to their big guns which were now spurting savagely.

Verdun and the Somme

Verdun is the Gettysburg of World War I. It didn't start off to be that big a fight; but before it was over the battle that started in February and ended in June had cost 600,000 casualties—slightly more of them French than German. Review the situation as the war entered its third year: the Germans had won some big, easy victories against the Russians. The Kaiser (left, reviewing troops) wondered why the same easy wins weren't to be had in the West where his armies were now commanded by General Erich von Falkenhayn—successor to von Moltke, the betrayer of The Plan. Falkenhayn knew that his enemies had more men than he did and that they died harder than the Russians. If he settled into a war of attrition, he would eventually wind up on the short end. Consequently, he laid on a small show—six German divisions against two French. The Germans had enormous artillery support and von Falkenhayn hoped for a breakthrough which would tear loose the entire front. On February 21, his shells started falling on the forts and trenches around the small city of Verdun. By the end of the month, some positions had been taken, some French had fled, and it looked like a break. But General Pétain was called and the reserves moved up.

Much of the German artillery blast (right above) had fallen on French African troops (right, below) who were dauntless on attack, but bad on defense and half-frozen in the European winter. The slimy, damp forts like Douamont were not their style. Re-enforcements thrown in held the line and by March the Germans were moving their attack west of Verdun on the other side of the Meuse River to flush out the artillery pounding their flank. Now, however, so many guns and troops had been poured in by both sides, that neither had the advantage. Though men bled and died in their thousands (following page, bottom) for wrinkles of ground like Dead Man Hill, the gains were nothing. By the end of June, the British were attacking to the west and Verdun was over. Note that the German attacks (following page, top) failed in spite of a gallantry quite as conspicuous as the French. A poilu wrote:

At every moment some part of the barricades blew up and the grenade duel resumed . . . We had installed machine guns which blocked up the gangwav and did splendid work . . . We had succeeded in checking the attack again, when the Boches started sending up petards which knocked us all down.

On July 1, 1916, the British attacked on a line running north from the Somme River. A bombardment had been going on since June 24; there were nearly 100,000 men in the assault. By the end of the day the gains they had made (following page) weren't worth talking about and there were 57,000 casualties, nearly 20,000 of them dead. Incredibly, Sir Douglas Haig kept at it until mid-November and before the thing was done had more than 400,000 casualties. Amazingly, his men stood it although they took hits from the moment they went over the top (left). A German said:

The intense bombardment was realized by all to be a prelude to the infantry assault at last. The men in the dugouts therefore waited ready, a belt full of hand grenades around them, gripping their rifles and listening for the bombardment to lift from the front defense zone onto the rear defenses. It was of vital importance to lose not a second in taking up position in the open and meeting the British infantry who would be advancing immediately behind the artillery barrage . . . At 7:30 A.M. the hurricane of shells ceased . . . the men at once went up the steep shafts . . . the machine guns were pulled out of dugouts.

Thus even the heaviest bombardment—though many of the British shells were faulty—and fine volunteer infantry were of no avail against men well dug in who kept their nerve. July 1, 1916, was the most disasterous day in the history of the British Army. The same German observer describes the slaughter that he witnessed:

A mass of shells from the German batteries in rear tore through the air and burst among the advancing lines. Whole sections seemed to fall and the rear formations, moving in closer order, quickly scattered. The advance rapidly crumpled under this hail of shells and bullets. All along the line men could be seen throwing their arms into the air and collapsing never to move again.

The dead (right) lay where they fell and it was clear that someone with more imagination than Douglas Haig would be needed to win this war. The Germans had been experimenting with infiltration tactics—small groups of men working forward, bypassing defended points and taking them from the rear. At Verdun, the system had some success. But the British too had been experimenting with a new weapon and it was now ready.

Very early in the war, a British lieutenant colonel, Ernest D. Swinton, had seen some American caterpillar tractors and figured that if you put a gun and some armor on one of them, you might have an answer to the machine gun. At first the only interested authority was Winston Churchill. By September 1916, though, Haig needed something to break the stalemate on the Somme. He was sent 49 tanks, but most of them broke down. Only 11 crept through a misty dawn on September 15 to fall upon the surprised Germans. One infantryman wounded in the attack said of the new gadget:

Wounded? Who cares about being wounded? There was that old D.16 groaning and grumbling along, poking her big nose here and there. She stopped now and then as if unsure of the road, and then plunged on over everything. I can still see her great head, coughing like a hippo. But the best of it was how the Tommies went on, following her— actually cheering! There hasn't been anything like her in this bloody war.

The German High Command agreed that "Certain facts cannot be denied . . . With a few improvements, this can become an exceedingly formidable weapon."

Thus 1916 came to an end on the Western Front and the troops settled down to a miserable winter in the trenches. It had been a year of slaughter. It would be another year before the tank was used properly and until then, men would go on being ordered into nineteenth-century assaults against twentieth-century defensive weapons. For the men in the trenches, however, the most pressing problem was not weaponry, but discomfort as represented by trench lice and mud (right). It was particularly bad on the northern end of the line and a great deal of discussion was devoted to just where the mud was thickest, slimiest, and nastiest. Siegfried Sassoon related:

The main characteristics of Camp 13 were smoke and mud. Mud was everywhere. All the company officers lived in one long, gloomy, draughty hut with an earth floor. Smoke was always drifting in from the braziers in the adjoining kitchen. After dark we sat and shivered in our "British warm" coats, reading, playing cards and writing letters with watering eyes by the feeble gleam of guttering candles . . . Orderlies brought in a clutter of tin mugs and plates and stew was consumed in morose discomfort.

{ **Who Won at Jutland?** }

The British Navy (left) was doing its job. German merchant shipping had been swept from the seas, the blockade was becoming ever tighter. By May of 1916, Admiral Reinhard Scheer, commanding the German High Sea Fleet, had made a decision. His fleet was smaller—244 main battery guns (11-inch or better) to the British 344. Scheer's plan called for luring the British Grand Fleet out, attacking it with submarines during the sortie and falling on a part of it during the confusion. Admiral Sir John Jellicoe knew that something was up and on the evening of May 30 set out from Scapa Flow to find the enemy. On May 31, the opposing cruiser squadrons, scouting ahead of the main forces, made contact and the Battle of Jutland began. At first it went well for the Germans. They pounded the British cruisers, which were silhouetted against the afternoon sky, until four British battleships came up and beat them back. Then quickly, the tide turned again as the German fleet steamed in from the south. At 6:15 in the evening, the two fleets met. Jellicoe maneuvered skillfully to cross Scheer's T; the latter turned his force away, then came on again. Again Jellicoe was across the T. Admiral Scheer was forced to retire again and the night fell.

Jellicoe did not press his enemy
(above) closely for a night action,
and Scheer slipped south and back
into port. Though the British lost
more ships and men, each side
claimed victory. Scheer said:

We have been able to prove to the
world that the English Navy no
longer possesses her boasted irresis-
tibility . . . If, however, we are not
finally to be bled to death, full use
must be made of the U-boat as a
means of war, so as to grip England's vital nerve.

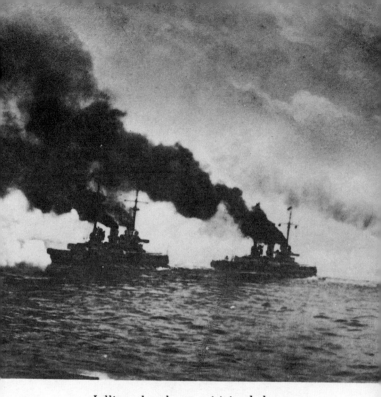

Jellicoe has been criticized, but perhaps he was wise not to overrisk his fleet. As Churchill said, he was the only man who could lose the war in an afternoon. Jellicoe wrote:

What are the facts? The High Sea Fleet (German) was steaming as fast as damaged ships could go for home behind the shelter of the minefields . . . One is forced to the conclusion that this "victorious" fleet did not consider itself capable of engaging only twelve of our British battleships.

Mountain
War

On the eastern fronts in 1916, the Italians continued to try to drive the Austrians (left) off the mountains and the Austrians had very much the best of it. Russia's response to Italy's appeals for help was to muster one more offensive. It was led by the able, if unpopular, Aleksei Brusilov and in June it fell upon the Austrians on a wide front east of Lemberg. Although supported by a mere 550 guns, it went well. Russian General Gourko, wrote:

The result of General Brusilov's advance passed all expectation. Evidently what afforded us the greatest help was that the Austrians did not expect such an attack at this time, especially on so wide a front.

Brusilov took 200,000 prisoners before the drive bogged down, and so impressed the Rumanians that they imprudently entered the war on the Allied side. A German-Austrian force smashed the new entry before the year was over. Gourko said:

There was no doubt that the public in the capital was both troubled and dissatisfied with the Government work in the interior . . . This affected the proper supplying of the Army . . . Many foresaw a Revolution when the war finished.

111

Woodrow Wilson was still trying to keep the United States neutral, but it was a losing proposition. Even though he had forced the Germans to suspend use of submarines against American ships there was a general popular sense that using submarines against any unarmed ship was not right. Vice-President Thomas Marshall noted that he was trying to obey the President's injunction to be neutral in word as well as deed, but added "I am the only American possessed of a voice who followed that request." The Army stepped up its recruiting effort (left) and Wilson himself made some speeches in favor of something vaguely called "preparedness." Nevertheless, the 1916 Democratic National Convention to renominate Wilson made peace its theme. Even William Jennings Bryan said:

I have differed with the President on some points of his policy of dealing with the great war, but I agree with the American people in thanking God we have a president who kept —who will keep—us out of war.

It became the slogan of the campaign (following page), but when Wilson was narrowly re-elected in November, "the war to end war" was just five months away.

VOTE FOR
WILSON
AND
MARSHALL
SEABURY
AND
McCOMBS
WOMEN'S BUREAU
DEMOCRATIC NATIONAL COMMITTEE
FOR
PRESIDENT
WOODROW
WILSON

"There Is
One
Choice
We Cannot
Make"

On January 31, 1917, Germany
turned from diplomacy and re-
turned to unrestricted submarine
warfare. Wilson read the German
note, commented "The break that
we have tried so hard to prevent
now seems inevitable," and severed
diplomatic relations with Germany.
Just a month later, American ire
went higher when it was discovered
that German Foreign Minister Alfred Zimmerman was trying to bring
Mexico into the war by promising
her Texas and Arizona. On March 9,
Wilson called for a special session of
Congress. Except for the formalities,
we were at war.

119

Woodrow Wilson rose before a cheering Congress (right) on April 2, 1917, and said:

We will not choose the path of submission . . . The world must be made safe for democracy . . . We shall fight for the things which we have always carried nearest to our hearts: for democracy, for the right of those who submit to authority to have a voice in their own governments, for the rights and liberties of small nations, for universal dominions of right by such a concert of free people as shall bring peace and safety to all nations and make the world itself at last free.

The crowds cheered; Wilson rode back to the White House, put his head down on his desk and burst into tears. A few sincere pacifists in the House and Senate fought the Declaration of War, but, on April 6, it was a fact and Wilson signed it. A draft law followed and on July 20, Secretary of War Newton D. Baker, blindfolded, reached into a fishbowl and pulled out number 258 (following page). `An army of civilians started on its way to training camps to supplement the tiny force of 92,-000 regulars we had ready to throw into the cauldron, and Wilson selected John Pershing to command.

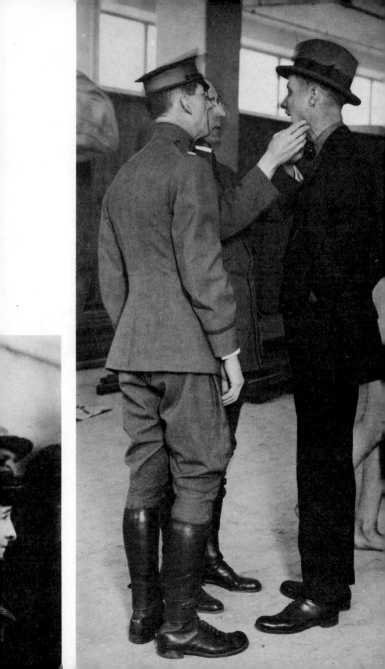

The draftee never has it good and the men of 1917 were no exception. They were marched out to drill on newly purchased plots of land which more often than not were unready to receive them (above). A Field Artilleryman at Camp Mills said:

Little provision had been made in this camp to meet the conditions of the fall weather of Long Island Sound. No adequate drainage facilities had been provided and as a result water ran down the company streets almost knee deep whenever there was a heavy rain storm . . .

and the cold, searching winds which blew off the Sound made life for the unaccustomed westerner very unpleasant. The tents in which the officers and men lived were far from satisfactory shelter against the cold wind . . . the enlisted men had to carry their food from the kitchen to their tents and ofttimes during a heavy storm much rain would be collected in their messkits and their food would be chilled . . . The officers and men were kept busy with drills of all kinds, including close order formations, nomenclature of the pistol and rifle and the 3-inch gun.

125

Attrition

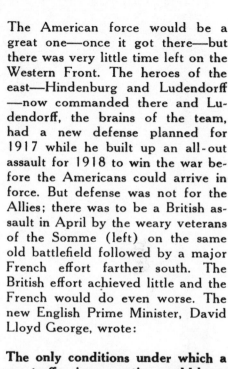

The American force would be a great one—once it got there—but there was very little time left on the Western Front. The heroes of the east—Hindenburg and Ludendorff —now commanded there and Ludendorff, the brains of the team, had a new defense planned for 1917 while he built up an all-out assault for 1918 to win the war before the Americans could arrive in force. But defense was not for the Allies; there was to be a British assault in April by the weary veterans of the Somme (left) on the same old battlefield followed by a major French effort farther south. The British effort achieved little and the French would do even worse. The new English Prime Minister, David Lloyd George, wrote:

The only conditions under which a great offensive operation could hope to succeed had been written in scarlet letters by the events of the war. It needed no special training or intelligence to read the warnings of past disaster . . . Haig, Robertson and Nivelle alike professes a conviction that the morale of the German Army had been shaken to such a degree by the raging fires of the Somme that its troops would no longer have the nerve to sustain a similar experience.

In the defense of Verdun, General Robert Nivelle (left, top) had done well and coined the phrase "They shall not pass!" Now, he was to be given a chance at an attack—the French half of the Allied spring thrust. The plan called for massive artillery support and a quick breakthrough by the infantry west of Reims. On April 16, it jumped off (following page) and from the start it was clear there would be no quick breakthrough. Until the end of the month, Nivelle kept on, gaining some ground. But the casualties were heavy (left, bottom), and they fell on a badly weakened French army. Mutinies broke out; 123 French soldiers were sentenced to death and 23 of them finally executed. As a fighting force the French were seriously undermined and if the Germans had fully grasped the situation they could have profited greatly. Novelist Humphrey Cobb tells of the slaughter:

Men started to scramble over the parapet, slipping, clawing, panting. Charpentier turned to lead the way. The next instant his decapitated body fell into his own trench . . . Three times 2nd Company tried to advance and each time the parapet was swept clean by the deadly machine gun fire.

The Yanks
Are
Coming

The first American combat forces in Europe were six little warships—Destroyer Division 8, commanded by Captain J. K. Taussig. They sailed from Boston with sealed orders and found they were to report to the senior British naval officer at Queenstown, in southern Ireland. German submarines had been sinking British shipping at a rate which would starve the British out before the year was over. Now, with the aid of the destroyers (left) and the introduction of a convoy system, the sub menace was beaten. An American left an account of the meeting:

A British officer . . . introduced Taussig to Bayly as the commander of the division and when the latter failed to make any reference pleasant or otherwise to the coming of our vessels I was astounded . . . Bayly's first words were these: "Captain Taussig, at what time will your vessels be ready for sea?" Taussig replied "I shall be ready when fueled." The admiral then asked, "Do you require any repairs?" Taussig answered, "No, sir." The admiral's third and last question was "Do you require any stores?" Taussig replied, "No, sir." The admiral concluded the interview with "You will take four days' rest. Good morning."

By the end of June, the American
Navy had brought its first troop convoy through successfully. The men
(right, top) landed at Saint-Nazaire,
then rattled across France in French
boxcars (right, bottom)—the famous 40 or 8's, 40 men or 8 mules
—to training areas. By the end of
the year there were four divisions in
France: 1st, 2nd, 26th (Yankee),
and 42nd (Rainbow). The 1st had
actually been in the line, but only in
a quiet sector for training. The winter of '17-'18 was a bitterly cold
one, but Pershing kept his men out-
doors. An officer recalled it:

Socks had to do duty as gloves, but
there was a shortage of socks. Shoes
had to be held together with rags
and strings. Billets were mere barns
—leaky, draughty, forbidding.
There were not enough stoves.
There was not enough good fire
wood. There were shortages of nearly everything. In those cold billets
it tried a man's soul to draw a razor
across his face. And there was nothing inspiring in the appearance of
the troops. Bristles on their faces,
vin rouge on their breaths, mud on
their long be-draggled overcoats,
their noses running and their chests
sore with coughing. They were neither beautiful to the eye nor consol-
ing to the spirit.

134

Revolution

In Russia, the long threatened revolution struck in March—a reluctant uprising of hungry people and troops tired of hopeless fighting (left). A New York Times correspondent reported:

The most phenomenal feature of the revolution was the swift and orderly transition whereby the control of the city passed from the regime of the old government into the hands of its opponents. The visible signs of revolution began on Thursday, March 8. Strikes were declared in several big munitions factories as a protest against the shortage of bread. Men and women gathered and marched through the streets, most of them in an orderly fashion. A few bread shops were broken into . . . Squads of mounted troops appeared, but through Thursday and Friday the utmost friendliness seemed to exist between the troops and the people . . . on Saturday, however, apparently without provocation the police were ordered to fire on the people . . . Until Sunday evening, however, there was no intimation that the affair would grow to the proportions of a revolution. The first serious outbreak came when the men of the Volynaky Regiment shot their officers and revolted when they received an order to fire upon striking workmen.

137

The March Revolution in Russia had replaced the Czar with a parliamentary government. In July, the new government launched an offensive under General Brusilov. At first, the Russians (right) made some gains, but in the face of a German-Austrian counterattack, they threw down their arms and ran (following page). The Bolsheviks, under Lenin, wanted to take Russia out of the war and the combination of their propaganda and the years of mishandling finished the Russian army. By September, there was no longer an Eastern Front; in November, the Bolsheviks seized the power. Germany would be able to use all her troops in the West. A Russian trooper told of the disintegration:

These meetings were always packed with our soldiers listening to revolutionary speeches . . . Some told the soldiers that they had nothing to gain and everything to lose by remaining . . . that their real enemies were not the Germans, but the landlords and the moneyed people, that it would be much better for them to go home and join in the fight against these people . . . The officers, with nearly all their power gone, hesitated even to gather together for fear they might be accused of conspiring against the men.

Caporetto
and
Cambrai

The first ally to taste the bitter fruit of Russian defeat was Italy. Seven German divisions were moved from the Eastern to the Italian front and on October 25, a joint German-Austrian assault struck the Italian line and smashed it (left). The Germans used new infiltration tactics with which they'd been experimenting in Russia and which they would use more extensively on the Western Front in 1918. Before it was over, the Italians had retreated some 70 miles, lost 600,000 men and eleven sorely needed French and British divisions had to be sent down to hold the line. Ernest Hemingway described the retreat from Caporetto:

"It's Germans that are attacking," one of the medical officers said. The word Germans was something to be frightened of. We did not want to have anything to do with Germans . . . The next night the retreat started. We heard that Germans and Austrians had broken through in the north and were coming down the mountains and valleys toward Cividale and Udine. The retreat was orderly, wet and sullen. In the night, going slowly along the crowded roads we passed troops marching under the rain, guns, horses pulling wagons, mules, motor trucks, all moving away from the front.

Before winter closed down the front, the British had one more try and it was a good one. Their enthusiastic young tank men found good tank country near Cambrai and for the first time the attack was to be made by a mass of tanks, not a handful. At dawn, November 20, they rolled out and it was finally clear to even the dullest that here was a weapon to deal with the machine gun. Substantial ground was gained with small losses. The Germans recaptured some of it, but a weapon to break the stalemate had been found. An officer recalled:

As far as the eye could see, monstrous tanks, like pre-historic animals were advancing relentlessly. Utterly bewildered the enemy was surrendering in panic in all directions. The noise inside "Hadrian" (the author's tank) was deafening it almost drowned the noise of the barrage and speech was practically impossible. The rattle of tracks and machinery produced an illusion of tremendous speed; but we were not moving faster than a mile an hour . . . the tanks were surrounded by groups of the enemy eager to surrender themselves and their arms.

During the winter, Hindenburg (left), the Kaiser (center), and Ludendorff (right) made their plans for the offensive which could not fail. Technically subordinate, Ludendorff was now in fact the designer. What he plotted was an assault against the British right. The Germans were to have a tremendous local superiority in men and guns. General Ludendorff wrote later in his memoirs:

The Army had thrown off the depressing effects of the previous year's fighting: its morale appeared completely restored, but in March, 1918, it could not be denied that secret agitation was making progress here and there . . . We hoped for success, even though they were no longer the troops of 1914, but only a kind of militia . . . The enemy was no better . . . What we should achieve, whether we should break through and start a war of movement or whether our effort should remain a sortie on a large scale was uncertain—like everything in war. I reported to the Emperor that the Army was well prepared to undertake the "biggest task in its history."

Obviously, Ludendorff was saying one thing to the Emperor and reserving some doubts to himself.

On March 21, the great offensive came and at first it went brilliantly (right). The opening—a stab at the point where the British and French lines met near Amiens—had been intended only as a feint. In fact, a hole was punched and it was April 5 before the front was stabilized. Ludendorff had taken 90,000 prisoners and inflicted tremendous losses. He had taken heavy losses himself, however, and when his real thrust came at the northern end of the British line he made big gains, but was stopped short of a breakthrough. A British infantryman has left an account of the assault (following page):

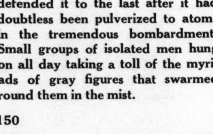

The machine gun system of defense on which we depended so much was absolutely useless in the thick mist that hid everything from view on that fatal morning. In a short while little groups of survivors down among the willow trees had been completely submerged: the troops in the sunken road we used to take to be our front line evidently defended it to the last after it had doubtless been pulverized to atoms in the tremendous bombardment. Small groups of isolated men hung on all day taking a toll of the myriads of gray figures that swarmed round them in the mist.

150

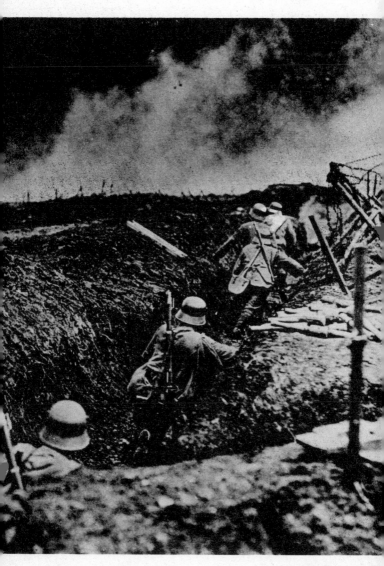

Frustrated, but by no means ready to give up, Ludendorff determined to try again on the French front around Soissons. Magnificent German staff work got the men and guns there in time for the assault to begin in the pre-dawn of April 25. The Germans used infiltration tactics—men going quickly ahead, bypassing rather than attacking strong points (below). This time the assault fell on badly positioned French troops supported by three worn out British divisions in for a rest. The front collapsed, the Germans raced through to the Marne only 50 miles

from Paris and to many it seemed that at last the real breakthrough had come. But Marshal Ferdinand Foch, belatedly appointed Allied Commander-in-Chief, remained cool:

From this time on, the Germans could no longer expect important results from the battle. In the face of the increased strength presented by the Allies, their attacks became more difficult and costly and they found themselves forced to stop.

In the lull, the Germans began to bombard Paris (following page).

France and Britain had been bled white by five years of fighting. Ever since America had entered the war, there had been great pressure for Americans to be put into French and British formations as replacements. General John J. Pershing (right) had no intention of agreeing to any such arrangement, but in the spring crisis Foch (left) tried once more. Again Pershing turned him down on piecemeal use of American manpower. In later years, he wrote:

After going over the whole situation again, they still insisted, whereupon I said with the greatest possible emphasis: "Gentlemen, I have thought this program over very deliberately and will not be coerced."

Then they compromised: Foch could use American troops by divisions as so long as the crisis lasted. The 1st Division took over a portion of the French line opposite the little village of Cantigny. The 3rd Division was ordered forward to stem the German assault on the Marne and its 7th Machine Gun Battalion. The 2nd Division—a peculiar outfit consisting of two regiments of Marines and two of Regular infantry—went northwest of Château-Thierry to stop the strong German attacks near Belleau Wood.

158

Counter-
Offensive

The 1st Division moved up to the Cantigny sector in camions (right) —open-top French trucks with wooden benches down each side. For the first month and a half they were there, the men of the 1st strung wire and connected the shell holes into a trench system. Then the orders came for the first American attack: the 28th Infantry Regiment of the 1st Division was to assault Cantigny itself. The village itself didn't amount to much, but its ruined buildings provided excellent cover for German artillery observers. A barrage from 386 guns began at 5:45 A.M. on May 28 and an hour later the men moved out supported by French tanks (following page). They made it into Cantigny. The division's history says:

During the hours preceding the assault there was little sleep or rest . . . At 5:45, the preparation for the attack began. With suddeness, every gun was directed upon its prescribed target. At 6:45, the 75's changed their fire to the rolling barrage . . . the infantry rose and advanced in three lines, following closely upon the barrage. During the preliminary bombardment tanks passed to the front line and accompanied the leading wave of infantry; there were surprisingly few casualties.

When the 2nd Division—Marines and infantry—was trucked up on May 30 to help hold the flank of the German push, a French officer expressed some doubts about their ability to do the job. "General," announced the division's chief of staff, "these are American Regulars. In a hundred and fifty years, they have never been beaten." The German push had stopped and the Marines were ordered to take Belleau Wood. One battalion attacked from the west and was cut to pieces by German machine guns. A second attacked from the south and just managed to get a toehold. For the

rest of June they fought. In the end they had the Wood—and it had cost 5711 casualties to do the job. John Thomason, a Marine turned writer, left an account of the fighting:

Combat groups of weary men . . . trudging forward. The sergeant beside the lieutenant stopped, looked at him with a frozen, foolish smile and crumpled into a heap of old clothes. Something took the kneecap off the lieutenant's right knee and his leg buckled under him. He noticed as he fell sideways that all about him his men were falling over like duck pins.

For the moment, Ludendorff was stopped. He would try once more, but the race to win before the Americans got into the line was lost. There were now 26 American divisions in France and they had shown they could fight, even though their inexperience led them to assault machine guns head on and take high casualties. They were also revealing officers of ability. The 1st Division's Operations Officer who had helped plan the assault on Cantigny was a colonel named George C. Marshall (above, standing) who would be U. S. Army Chief of Staff in World War II. And in the 42nd (Rainbow) Division they had an Executive Officer who wore a cap with no stiffener and went on trench raids armed with a riding crop: General Douglas MacArthur (right), the conqueror-to-be of Japan.

Ludendorff made one more try. It was a two-pronged attempt to get over the Marne. One thrust came in the Château-Thierry area, the other farther east past Reims. There were three American divisions in line with the French: the 3rd at Château-Thierry, the 28th (National Guard division from Pennsylvania) farther over, and at the eastern end of the line, the 42nd (Rainbow). On the night of July 14-15, the attack came and crossed the river near Château-Thierry except where it ran into the 3rd Division's 38th Infantry. The 38th fought from behind a railway embankment (left) and would not be moved. Farther east, the 42nd Division was part of a yielding defense. The old front line was virtually given up. Behind it lay strong points held by sacrifice squads, then two defense lines. It worked—artillery lashed the Germans as they struggled through the strong points and they got nowhere against the main defense line. A Rainbow man remembered it:

The fire here was so severe that time after time men had to be dug out of the trench where they had been completely covered . . . As in the grasp of a great hurricane that tears and pulls, the trees above them were being twisted and battered.

For all his exertions, Ludendorff was now in a deep, rather narrow pocket jutting into the Allied position. No sooner had the last German push of July 15 failed than Foch went over to the offensive himself. It was to be a joint American (left)-French attack on the west side of the pocket —approximately from Soissons to Château-Thierry. Just south of Soissons, the American 1st and 2nd Divisions with the 1st French Moroccan Division between them were to drive east and cut the best road out of the pocket. Farther down, the 4th, 26th, and 3rd Divisions were in with other French divisions to push the Germans back over the Marne and north. On July 18, French General Charles Mangin said "Go." The 1st and 2nd had spent most of the night before marching to the front in a torrential rainstorm. A division historian said:

At command, the men slung and adjusted their battle packs and the columns moved out . . . so black was the night that they could not see each other and contact was maintained by having each man place his hand on the man in his front. Scarcely had the columns strung out than a storm broke of tropical violence . . . The rain poured in torrents, soaking the clothing and the packs.

At Soissons, the early going was so good that the French decided to try a cavalry attack (left) which the Germans cut to ribbons. By the second day, though, the road was cut in spite of tremendous casualties. An American officer wrote later:

We all realized that more of us would be going west . . . the fields through which we advanced were already sprinkled with the wreckage of our battalion's attack. The less severely wounded stumbled to the rear, others lay out pleading for help or first aid, a few merely raised tired heads to see us go by and then sank back in silence. Give me the front line where a fellow doesn't have to wade through the ghastly results of an assault . . . I had never dreamed of worse barrage . . . The first person I recognized was Becker. He was moving the second wave forward. He turned, grinned and waved a greeting. He took one step towards me and then disappeared. A terrific explosion, a sharp pain, a struggle to breathe the burnt up air and I was down. A long pronged icicle drove deep into my flesh. The ice melted into molten fire which spread slowly up one side of my body. I was wounded and it hurt. But I had a ticket back to the rear— and to safety.

If the progress around Soissons was quick, dramatic, and costly, the divisions pushing from the bottom of the pocket found themselves in a dirty fight. The ground north of the Marne gets higher, so the attackers had the enemy looking down their throats. The first divisions crossed the Marne, but the Germans simply fell back to another good position behind a creek-sized river called the Ourcq. The 42nd and the 28th Divisions relieved the starters and ran up fearful casualty lists (right) getting over the Ourcq. Back went the Germans behind the Vesle River and the 4th and the 32nd Divisions exhausted themselves trying to get over it. The pocket was gone —the line now ran straight from Soissons to Reims, but the Germans had made an excellent defense of it. John Dos Passos, who drove an ambulance, wrote of the price one doughboy paid:

"Be careful of my leg, can't yer:" he found himself whining over and over again . . . And he was jolting and swinging about in the stretcher, clutching hard with his hands at the poles of the stretcher. The pain in his legs grew worse . . . He fought against the desire to groan, but at last he gave in and lay lost in the monotonous singsong of his groans.

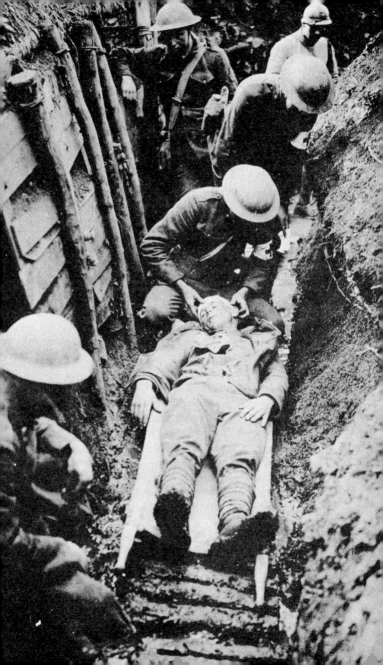

The tiny air forces with which everyone had begun the war had now grown into elaborate affairs with training fields (above) and missions which included bombing and strafing in support of ground troops as well as the earlier dog fights. In April 1918 the war's greatest ace—Baron von Richthofen, with 80 victories—was shot down and killed either by a young Canadian pilot or by an Australian antiaircraft gunner. The accounts of his last flight are conflicting and even the most painstaking researchers are unable to say certainly who did for "The Red

Knight." The sky had become a new battleground. Edwin C. Parsons tells the following story of an encounter over the lines:

I was overanxious and started to open fire from at least a half mile away . . . They scattered like a covey of quail. Then I dived right into the middle of the formation. In my ignorance, I thought I could pick off a couple . . . I didn't even come close to getting one . . . They had me surrounded on every side. I suddenly changed from a bold marauder of the skies into a very scared youth.

175

176

The first Americans to get into the air war managed it by enlisting in the French Foreign Legion and then forming the famed Lafayette Escadrille which first went into action in April 1916. Many of these adventurous young men (left; top) were dead or invalided by the time America entered the war; most of the rest transferred to the American Air Service. In spite of the fact that they spent the war flying planes borrowed from the French and British, the Americans produced some outstanding pilots. Eddie Rickenbacker (below, left) was the leader with 26 victories. Raoul Lufbery (below, center), the finest of the Escadrille pilots, made a brilliant record before he was killed in May 1918. In Colonel William Mitchell (below, right), the Americans had a great, if intemperate, exponent of air power. Mitchell had his boys shower this leaflet on the infantry:

From the American Scrappers in the Air to the American Scrappers on the Ground:
Doughboys: While you are giving the Boche hell on the ground, we are helping you to the limit in the air. . . . Use us to the limit, show your panels, burn your signal lights, wave a cloth, anything to tell us where you are and what you need.

On August 8, the British, aided by the French on their right flank, attacked east of Amiens. The Canadian Corps, well supported by tanks, spearheaded and their gain for the day was an astonishing seven miles. What the English like to call The Hundred Days (actually there would be only 96) had begun. From here on Foch would attack steadily. Sometimes German troops crumbled, far more often they fought hard although the Allies knew from prisoners (left) that German Army morale was poor. Nor were conditions much better on the home front. Hans Hanssen noted:

I asked Dr. Friedegg how conditions were in Austria. "They are terrible in every respect," he answered. "Only one pound of potatoes per person is distributed per week."

Of Berlin the same writer said:

When I was going towards Unter den Linden this evening, a mysteriously heavy and oppressive atmosphere was hovering over the large cafes. A dense crowd was pressed together outside the telegraph room of Lokal Anzeiger to read the latest telegrams. "How pitiful it is," an unknown man said to me as I walked.

On August 20, the French under Mangin attacked north of Soissons and moved well. Another British push on the 23rd gained ground; Ludendorff knew he was in trouble and pulled back all along the front. Foch kept after him, back over the old battlefields (right) and by early September, Ludendorff had to pull back again, this time to the Hindenburg line, a system of concrete pillboxes and defenses in depth. Even against weakening resistance, it was going to be a costly position to crack. Foch was full of optimism. He wrote Haig:

The enemy has everywhere been shaken by the blows already dealt him. We must repeat these blows without losing any time; and to increase their effect we must use every division that can be put into the line without delay. Therefore I assume that the attack of your Third Army, postponed already until August 21, will be launched on that day with the utmost violence. After your brilliant successes . . . any hesitation on your part would not accord with the situation of the enemy and the moral ascendancy we have obtained over him.

The British did well and the French continued to move ahead.

There were now enough trained divisions in France for Pershing to have the army he had waited so long for. Foch made one last effort to have them distributed, but Pershing settled the matter for good by replying:

"Marshal Foch, you may insist all you please, but I decline absolutely to agree with your plans. While our army will fight wherever you decide, it will not fight except as an independent American army."

Foch decided that it could best fight to wipe out the Saint-Mihiel salient, the big bulge into the Allied line east of Verdun. Pershing put seven divisions on one side of the bulge, one division on the other while the French filled in around the tip. At 1 A.M. on September 12, the artillery started and at 5 A.M., after waiting out the barrage, the American Army (left) made its first attack. It went beautifully. Prisoners started coming in very early. By dark the converging forces from opposite sides of the bulge were only seven miles apart. Pershing kept them moving all night and at 6 A.M. on the 13th, the 1st and Yankee Divisions linked up. It was John J. Pershing's birthday and he called it "a very happy one."

The End
in
the East

Since 1915 the British and the French had had a force in Greece. It had come originally to help rescue the Serbian army and a very ticklish business it was; Greece was not yet in the war, but her Premier did agree to let the Allies pass through. While the Greek King and Premier bickered, the visitors stayed. Now they were re-enforced by the rugged Serbian troops, rested and refitted and led by a good French general, Louis Franchet d'Esperey. The Serbians wanted to attack north, rout the Bulgarians (left) and get back to Serbia. On September 15, they went, and with the Serbs fighting ferociously Bulgaria quit. A London dispatch gives some of the flavor:

The Bulgarians are completely defeated, are in flight in Macedonia and are burning stores and villages . . . New regiments thrown in by the Bulgarians were forced to retreat with the others. Serbian troops are pursuing them night and day. The allied troops have now advanced more than twelve miles and their progress is so rapid that they have not been able to count the prisoners . . . they have taken the towns of Topolets, Poshista, Beshnista, Mellynista, Vitolishtic, Rasimbay and the heights of Kuchkov Kamera.

Turkey was the next Entente power to go. The British put a strong force under General Sir Edmund "The Bull" Allenby in Egypt and he drove into Palestine while Lawrence of Arabia rallied the Arabs to harry the Turkish flank. At Megiddo, Allenby broke the Turkish line with infantry, then sent Australian (left) and Indian cavalry thundering through a hole in the Turkish right flank. It turned into a rout and Turkey threw in the sponge. General Archibald Wavell reported:

On other occasions during the War, in France or elsewhere, the horsemen had always come too soon or too late . . . Now at last, thanks to good staff work and bold handling, the cavalry went cleanly through almost on the heels of the assaulting infantry . . . As the leading regiment, the 2nd Lancers of the Indian cavalry, shook itself clear of the hills early next morning met a Turkish battalion which had been sent to hold the pass and promptly charged it with the lance. The shock of surprise at meeting cavalry at such an unexpected time and place was probably too much for the enemy's nerves and musketry; the fire was so wild that there was only one Indian casualty, while some fifty of the Turks were speared.

As the end of the summer approached, the Germans (right) braced for the final blows. Both the Kaiser and his generals knew all was lost, but they hung on hoping that they might be able to blunt and bloody the attacks. By showing strength they hoped to get a settlement in which the generals could keep their armies and the Kaiser could keep his throne for another try another day. But the British blockade had done its job well; both the Germans at home and the troops in the field were weakened by bad food and too little of it. Though the army did not ever truly break, it fought with little heart and less hope. Only in isolated instances did the German soldier not do his duty to the end. Erich Maria Remarque reported the mood in a great novel, All Quiet on the Western Front:

Summer of 1918—Never was so much silently suffered as in the moment when we departed again for the frontline. Wild tormenting rumors of an armistice and peace are in the air . . . Never was life in the line more bitter or more full of horror than in the hours of the bombardment when the blanched faces lie in the dirt and the hands clutch at one thought: No! No! Not now! Not now at the last moment!

The Last Stand

The British attacks (above) jumped off on September 27. It was a three-army affair and insofar as there were enough tanks to go around, the tactics were based on the success at Cambrai the year before: short artillery preparation, surprise, maximum tank support for the infantry. It is a measure of the decline of the German soldier that the British made excellent progress although the forces involved were about even. In the past a marked numerical superiority was considered essential for success. A smaller British-Belgian drive around the old killing ground of Ypres bogged down in the famous Flanders mud. Austral-

ian General Sir John Monsash, who commanded his own Aussies plus two borrowed American divisions during the push, wrote:

From now on for the next 48 hours I undertake the heavy artillery bombardment . . . of the main Hindenburg Line with over a thousand guns.

An English war correspondent said of the results of the bombardment:

I saw many batches of prisoners coming back . . . with wet chalk on their uniforms, but chalk no whiter than the faces of these men who had been under two days of constant bombardment and had been almost maddened by it.

For their part, the Americans (above) were to attack from the Meuse River over to the Argonne Forest. The main French assault would be on their left. Pershing had used veterans at Saint-Mihiel. Thus, seven of the nine outfits that crept up to the jump-off positions on the night of September 25 were green. At 5:30 A.M. they went over (following pages). A private wrote:

We went over the top! But it was different from what I thought it would be. I expected all of us to rise and start at the same time. But

we didn't. There was a low embankment around the trench where we
were located. Finally a man was
beckoning to my squad and mutter-
ing to the other boys "Well, I guess
we'd better go." I started forward.
The other boys went alongside.
When we came to our big burly
corporal he was in tears; he could
not go for he was wounded. So we
three set out without a leader, but
just as we were surmounting the embankment, Rake, the man on my
left stiffened and fell heavily. I
thought almost flippantly, "Poor fellow, he is dead."

The French attack west of the Argonne was moving and on the American front things were going surprisingly well (above, infantrymen take cover from shelling; at right, French tank and dead German). The first important objective was Montfaucon, a village on steep, high ground in the middle of the front. The French had said Pershing wouldn't take it that winter. Pershing hoping to get it the very first day, did so on the second. On the third day, though, the push started to run out of gas. The ground was torn up from earlier fighting; moving artil-

lery, food, and ammunition was a slow business and just to make it worse, it had been raining since the drive began. Casualties had been high—one division lost two-thirds of its riflemen. Pershing decided to pause and consolidate. William March left a record of the fighting:

A fellow named Fallon . . . went off his nut. He got up on the parapet . . . during a barrage and nobody could coax him in. "I want to get shot," he kept saying; "I know perfectly well what I'm doing. I want to get myself shot."

With the British (left), French and Americans all gaining ground almost daily Berlin finally acted. Early in October, the first message went to Woodrow Wilson: "The German Government requests the President of the United States . . . to take steps for the restoration of peace . . ." Wilson replied via Secretary of State Lansing that Germany could have an armistice if she withdrew her troops from foreign soil. France and Britain were not settling so easily. They informed Wilson that the only armistice they'd agree to was one in which the German army gave up its arms. The American man in the street would have considered the terms much too mild—most people felt that the only really proper ending to this war would be a public hanging of the Kaiser. An editorial in The New York Times is characteristic:

The Germans have not yet learned to understand, much less to speak, the language of agreement. We may regard their latest note as an effort to meet the President's demands. The change we note in Germany is not in her Constitution . . . she is hopeless of victory . . . it remains for them not to choose the terms, but to accept whatever terms may be imposed upon them.

On the Meuse-Argonne front, Pershing was ready to try again, this time with his best divisions. On October 4 they jumped off—but made no progress. They were up against the main German line of resistance, a series of hill lines which constituted the toughest terrain anywhere along the front. 'German artillery on the hills in the Argonne and on the heights across the Meuse River flogged the American flanks. On October 11, Pershing took measures. The American Second Army was formed to operate east of the Meuse and clear the heights. French Premier Georges Clemenceau, who al-

ways had thought Pershing too up-pity, even tried to get Pershing fired, but Foch put his foot down. Throughout October, we hacked away, getting small gains and large casualty lists. Fresh divisions came in to relieve the exhausted men (below). A 4th Division man wrote:

Soon the darkness in the thick woods became almost impenetrable. The men in the front lines fell. The men behind stumbled over their dead or wounded comrades . . . They could not see . . . the advance stopped . . . the word was passed along to withdraw.

If October was a tough month for Pershing, it did make two other Americans famous. The 77th Division fighting in the Argonne Forest was largely composed of New York City draftees or what their commander called "a group of hardy frontiersmen from the Bowery and the Lower East Side." A battalion of these city slickers moved ahead of its mates and the Germans cut it off. It promptly became known as the Lost Battalion and under Major Charles Whittlesey fought for a week with no food and very little water until it was relieved. Out of 650 men, there were only 194 who didn't require hospitalization. An even greater popular hero was Corporal Alvin York (left), a big, red-headed Tennesseean. He'd overcome religious scruples and, in October, he was part of a 21-man patrol that was bushwhacked in the Argonne. Suddenly York was the only noncom left and the machine guns that had ruined the patrol were still shooting. York had nothing but his rifle, but he was a crack shot and picked off the machine gunners so successfully that the Germans started surrendering. York came back with 132 prisoners, one of them a major, and he left 25 dead men at the scene of his fight. York said, "I wanted to do the best I could."

On October 31 Pershing prepared for his third try at the German positions. The French and the British were moving steadily ahead and he was determined not to be out of the victory parade. At 5:30 A.M. on November 1, seven divisions went over the top and suddenly all the bitter attrition of October had its reward. The center of the line, with the 2nd Division leading he way, moved ahead five miles on the very first day. On the second day they were still going, swinging northeast to the line of the Meuse River and by now the 2nd Division was doing so well that it went ahead in marching rather than battle order. Then as the front moved up, happy French (left) came out to greet troops moving fast through fading German resistance (below).

In Germany events were moving quickly. Ludendorff had resigned. The German Navy had planned to go out for a finish fight with the British Grand Fleet, but the sailors had mutinied. A somewhat liberalized government had been installed, but now crowds in the street demonstrated for a Republic. The Kaiser, who still couldn't face the fact that he was through, put troops in the streets (left) to head off a revolution. Hindenburg told him that even the army couldn't keep him in power; Wilhelm finally saw the light and left for Holland. The home situation is reflected in a statement by a member of the German delegation, as quoted by Foch:

Immediately after this Herr Erzberger requested that military operations be at once suspended. He gave as a reason the disorganization and lack of discipline which reigned in the German Army and the spirit of revolution that was spreading through Germany as a consequence of the people's sufferings . . . All these circumstances led him to fear that Germany might soon fall into the grip of Bolshevism and once central Europe was invaded by this scourge, western Europe, he said, would find the greatest difficulty in escaping from it.

The German armistice negotiators, led by a round, formal looking politician named Matthias Erzberger, had been told by Foch to cross into the French lines near Cambrai. Retreating Germans filled the roads. Once across, the representatives were sent to the forest of Compiègne. On November 8, Foch met them as the head of the Allied delegation (right). Erzberger asked what the armistice provisions were; Foch asked if that meant he was asking for an armistice. Erzberger said he was. . . . The end on the American 4th Division's front was typical:

On the eleventh hour of the eleventh day of the eleventh month peace settled over war-scarred Europe. The smoke from the cannon ceased, the machine guns ate up no more tape. Only the inevitable transport moved. It was the Sabbath of Mars. That night, all along the front, a weird display of Very lights, rockets and burning powder turned darkness into day and gave the impression of some gigantic 4th of July celebration.

Foch issued a general order:

You have won the greatest battle in history and rescued the most sacred of causes — the Liberty of the World.

210

The war had lasted a little more than four years and three months. It is impossible to say how many men were killed, but ten million is a conservative estimate. America paid only a small part of the bill—116,516 dead, about half of them battle casualties. The victors came to Paris to write a peace treaty to keep it all from happening again. There, amid the splendors of the Hall of Mirrors, ended the Great War. But the stage had already been set for an even greater holocaust. Within months a fanatical splinter group, later to be called the Nazi Party, had held its first meeting in a Munich beer cellar; within ten years the Japanese were pillaging China; within fifteen, Mussolini's legions had smashed into Ethiopia. The war to make the world safe for democracy was followed by the greatest upsurge of totalitarianism the world had ever endured. The victorious Allies, after surrendering Spain, Austria and Czechoslovakia, reluctantly drew the line at Poland. There, a scant twenty years after Versailles, Hitler's panzers finally shattered the uneasy peace; the war to end all war had won little more than a prolonged armistice.

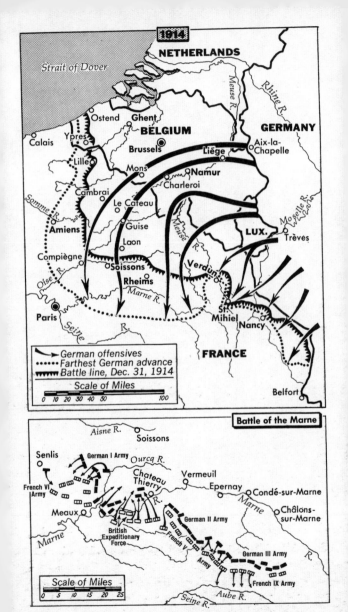

1914

Strait of Dover

NETHERLANDS

BELGIUM

GERMANY

Ostend · Ghent

Calais · Ypres

Brussels · Liège · Aix-la-Chapelle

Lille · Mons · Namur

Cambrai · Charleroi

Le Cateau

Amiens · Guise · LUX. · Trèves

Compiègne · Laon · Verdun

Soissons · St. Mihiel

Paris · Rheims · Nancy

FRANCE

Belfort

➤ German offensives
••••• Farthest German advance
⋀⋀⋀ Battle line, Dec. 31, 1914

Scale of Miles
0 10 20 30 40 50   100

Battle of the Marne

Aisne R. · Soissons

Senlis · German I Army · Ourcq R.

French VI Army · Chateau Thierry · Vermeuil · Epernay · Condé-sur-Marne

Meaux · R. · Marne · Châlons-sur-Marne

British Expeditionary Force · German II Army

French V Army

German III Army

Marne · French IX Army

Seine R. · Aube R.

Scale of Miles
0   5   10   15   20   25

EASTERN FRONT: 1914-1916

Stockholm
SWEDEN
Baltic Sea
Marienburg
Tannenberg
Vilna
Moscow
Minsk
Masurian Lakes
GERMANY
Vistula R.
Warsaw
Brest-Litovsk
R U S S I A
Tarnow
Gorlice
Lemberg
Kiev
Dnieper R.
Don R.
Danube R.
Vienna
CARPATHIAN
Budapest
MTS.
Odessa
AUSTRIA-HUNGARY
RUMANIA
Black Sea
MONTE-NEGRO
Belgrade
Bucharest
Danube R.
SERBIA
Cetinje
Sofia
BULGARIA
ALBANIA
DARDANELLES
GREECE

→ *Russian offensive, 1914*
⇢ *German offensive, 1915*
→ *Brusilov offensive, 1916*
····· *Farthest Russian advance*
·•·•· *Farthest German advance*

Scale of Miles
0   100   200   300   400   500

Dardanelles Campaign

Aegean Sea
Sea of Marmara
Gallipoli
Suvla Bay
CAPE SUVLA
DARDANELLES
Galata
Cardak
Lapseki
Beyçayiri
IMBROZ I.
Anzac Cove
Maidos
Chanak
OTTOMAN EMPIRE
Turkish minefields
CAPE HELLES
Erenkoy
Kum Kale

→ *Allied landings from April 25 to Aug. 6*
····· *Final Allied gains*

Scale of Miles
0   2   4   6   8   10

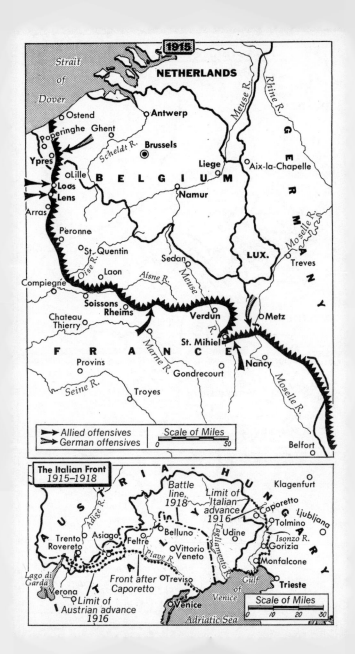

1915

Strait
of
Dover

NETHERLANDS

Rhine R.

Meuse R.

Ostend
Antwerp
Poperinghe Ghent
Scheldt R.
Brussels
Ypres
Liege
Aix-la-Chapelle
oLille
BELGIUM
Loos
Lens
Namur
Arras

Peronne
Sedan
LUX.
Treves

St. Quentin
Oise R.
Laon
Aisne R.
Moselle R.
Meuse

Compiegne

Soissons
Rheims
Verdun
Metz
Chateau
Thierry
R.
St. Mihiel
Marne R.
FRANCE
Provins
Nancy
Gondrecourt

Seine R.
Troyes
Moselle R.

G E R M A N Y

➤ Allied offensives
➤➤ German offensives

Scale of Miles
0   50

Belfort

**The Italian Front
1915–1918**

A U S T R I A - H U N G A R Y

Klagenfurt

Adige R.
Battle
line,
1918
Limit of
Italian
advance
1916
Caporetto
Ljubljana
Tolmino

Trento
Rovereto
Asiago
Feltre
Belluno
Udine
Isonzo R.
Gorizia

Lago di
Garda
Piave R.
oVittorio
Veneto
Tagliamento
Monfalcone

Verona
Front after
Caporetto
Treviso
Gulf
of
Venice
Trieste

I T A L Y

Limit of
Austrian advance
1916
Venice
Adriatic Sea

Scale of Miles
0   10   20   30

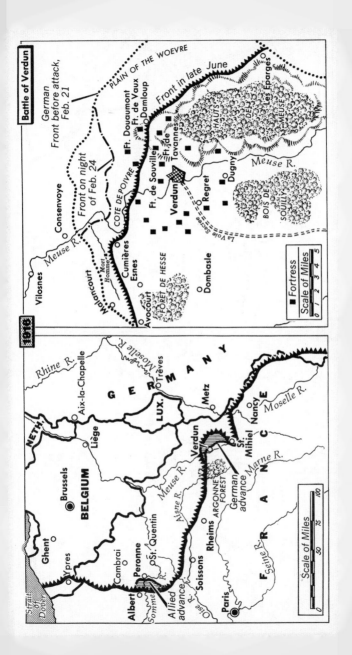

Battle of Verdun

PLAIN OF THE WOEVRE

German Front before attack, Feb. 21

Front in late June

Consenvoye

Front on night of Feb. 24

Vilosnes

Meuse R.

Molancourt

Mort Homme

COTE DE POIVRE

Cumières

Esnes

Avocourt

FORÊT DE HESSE

Dombasle

Ft. Douaumont

Ft. de Vaux

Damloup

Ft. de Tavannes

Ft. de Souville

Verdun

Regret

Dugny

HAUTS DE MEUSE

Les Eparges

Meuse R.

BOIS DE SOUILLY

La Voie Sacrée

■ Fortress

Scale of Miles

0 1 2 3 4 5

1918

Rhine R.

Moselle R.

NETH.

Aix-la-Chapelle

GERMANY

Liège

LUX.

Trèves

Metz

BELGIUM

Brussels

Ghent

Ypres

Strait of Dover

Cambrai

Péronne

St. Quentin

Somme R.

Albert

Allied advance

Oise R.

Aisne R.

Soissons

Rheims

ARGONNE FOREST

Meuse R.

Verdun

German advance

St. Mihiel

Nancy

Moselle R.

F R A N C E

Marne R.

Paris

Seine R.

Scale of Miles

0 25 50 75 100

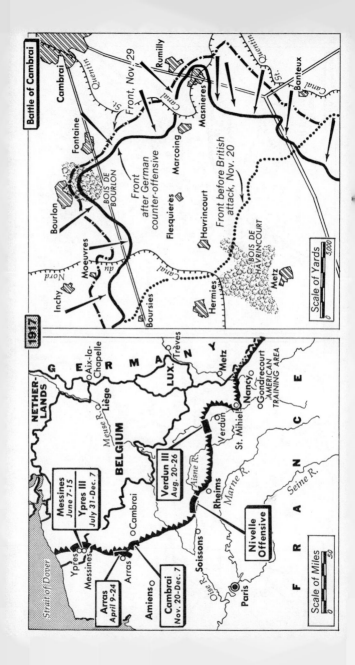

Battle of Cambrai

Cambrai

Quentin

Front, Nov. 29

Rumilly

Quentin

St.

Banteux

Canal

Fontaine

Canal

Masnieres

BOIS DE
BOURLON

Marcoing

*Front
after German
counter-offensive*

Bourlon

Flesquières

*Front before British
attack, Nov. 20*

Moeuvres

Havrincourt

Canal du Nord

Inchy

BOIS DE
HAVRINCOURT

Metz

Boursies

Hermies

Canal

Scale of Yards
0   5,000

1917

NETHER-
LANDS

G E R M A N Y

Aix-la-
Chapelle

Trèves

Meuse R.

Liège

LUX.

Metz

BELGIUM

Nancy

Verdun

Gondrecourt

St. Mihiel

AMERICAN
TRAINING AREA

Ypres
Messines

Cambrai

Arras

Aisne R.

Rheims

F R A N C E

Strait of Dover

Amiens

Oise R.

Soissons

Marne R.

Seine R.

Paris

Messines
June 7-15
Ypres III
July 31-Dec. 7

Verdun III
Aug. 20-26

Arras
April 9-24

Cambrai
Nov. 20-Dec. 7

**Nivelle
Offensive**

Scale of Miles
0   50

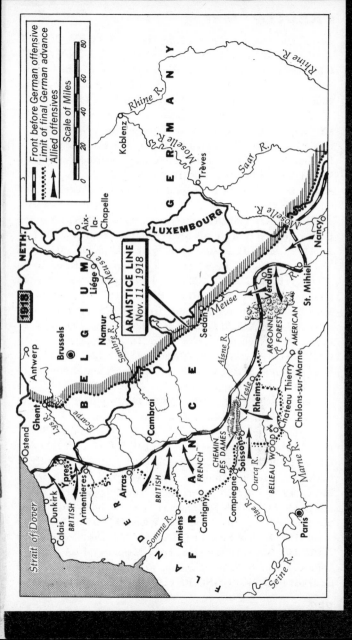

NETH.

Strait of Dover

1918

Ostend
Antwerp
Ghent
Brussels

B E L G I U M

Namur
Liége
Aix-la-Chapelle

LUXEMBOURG

G E R M A N Y

Koblenz
Trèves
Saar R.
Rhine R.
Moselle R.

Calais
Dunkirk
Ypres
Armentieres
Arras
Cambrai

Lys R.
Scarpe R.
Meuse R.
Sambre R.

ARMISTICE LINE
Nov. 11, 1918

Sedan
Meuse R.

Verdun
Moselle R.
Nancy
St. Mihiel

F L A N D E R S

F R A N C E

Amiens
Somme R.
Cantigny
Compiegne
Oise R.
CHEMIN DES DAMES
Soissons
Ourcq R.
BELLEAU WOOD
Chateau Thierry
Chalons-sur-Marne
Marne R.

FRENCH
BRITISH

Aisne R.
Rheims
Vesle R.
ARGONNE FOREST
AMERICAN

Paris
Seine R.
Rhine R.

Front before German offensive
Limit of final German advance
Allied offensives

Scale of Miles
0   20   40   60   80

CREDITS / text

18-19 The London Times; from THE HISTORY OF THE TIMES / **20-21** Same / **24-25** From THE PERSONAL MEMOIRS OF JOFFRE, Harper & Row, 1932 / **24-25** The London Times; from THE HISTORY OF THE TIMES / **30-31** Sir John French; from 1914, Houghton Mifflin, 1919 / **34-35** W. W. Eaton; from "A Serbian Diary," ATLANTIC MONTHLY, May, 1916 / **36-37** Hans Hanssen; from DIARY OF A DYING EMPIRE, translated by Oscar Winther, University of Indiana Press, 1955 / **38-39** Maj. Gen. Sir Alfred Knox; from WITH THE RUSSIAN ARMY 1914-1917, Dutton, 1921 / **46-47, 50-51** Col. A. F. Duguid; from OFFICIAL HISTORY OF THE CANADIAN FORCES IN THE GREAT WAR, Minister of National Defense, Ottawa, 1919 / **52-55** Sir Philip Gibbs; from NOW IT CAN BE TOLD, Harper & Row, 1920 / **58-59** Barbara Tuchman; from THE GUNS OF AUGUST, Macmillan, 1962 / **60-63** Maj. Gen. Sir Alfred Knox; from WITH THE RUSSIAN ARMY 1914-1917 / **66-67** Sir Winston Churchill; from THE WORLD CRISIS 1916-1918, Scribner's, 1927 / **68-69** Aubrey Herbert; from MONS, ANZAC AND KUT, Edward Arnold Publishers, Ltd., London, 1919 / **70-71** Henry W. Nevinson; from THE DARDENELLES CAMPAIGN, Holt, Rinehart and Winston, 1919 / **72-73** Lt. Milutin Krunish; from SERBIA CRUCIFIED, Houghton Mifflin, 1918 / **78-79** Walter Raleigh; from THE WAR IN THE AIR, Clarendon Press, Oxford, 1922 / **80-81** H. A. Jones; from THE WAR IN THE AIR, Clarendon Press, Oxford, 1928 / **82-83** Frederick Oughton; from THE ACES, Putnam's, 1916 / **84-85** Edwin C. Parsons; from I FLEW WITH THE LAFAYETTE ESCADRILLE, E. C. Seale, 1963 / **86-87** Capt. Ernst Lerhmann, Howard Mingnons; from THE ZEPPELINS, Dodd, Mead, 1927 / **92-93** Henry Bourdeaux; from THE LAST DAYS OF FORT VAUX, Thomas Nelson & Sons Ltd / **96-97** Sir Winston Churchill, from THE WORLD CRISIS 1916-1918 / **102-103** Arch Whitehouse; from TANK, Doubleday, 1960 / **104-105** Siegfried Sassoon; from Memoirs of an Infantry Officer, Faber & Faber, London, 1931 / **110-111** Gen. Basil Gourko; from WAR AND REVOLUTION IN RUSSIA, Macmillan, 1919 / **126-127** From THE BATTERY BOOK: A HISTORY OF BATTERY A 306 F.A., DeVinne Press, 1921 / **128-129** David Lloyd George; from WAR MEMOIRS, Little Brown, 1934 / **130-31** Humphrey Cobb; from PATHS OF GLORY, Viking Press / **134-135** Reprinted from "Proceedings" by permission; © 1922 by U. S. Naval Institute / **136-137** Col. E. S. Johnston; from AMERICANS VS. GERMANS, The Infantry Journal Press / **138-139** Capt. D. E. Hickey; from ROLLING INTO ACTION, Hutchinson & Co., London / **140-141** Nahum Sabsay; from A MOMENT OF HISTORY — A RUSSIAN SOLDIER IN THE FIRST WAR, Caxton Press, Caldwell, Ohio, 1960; © Nahum Sabsay / **144-145** Ernest Hemingway; from A FAREWELL TO ARMS, Scribner's, 1929 / **148-149** From THE MEMOIRS OF GENERAL ERICH LUDENDORF, Hutchinson & Co., London / **150-151** Aubrey Smith; from FOUR YEARS ON THE WESTERN FRONT, Odhams Press Ltd., London, 1922 / **154-155** from THE MEMOIRS OF MARSHAL FOCH, Doubleday, 1931 / **158-159** John J. Pershing; from MY EXPERIENCES IN THE WORLD WAR, Lippincott, 1931 / **160-161** From HISTORY OF THE FIRST DIVISION, Holt, Rinehart and Winston, 1931 / **162-163** Capt. John Thomason; from FIX BAYONETS, Scribner's / **166-167** Henry J. Reilly; from AMERICANS ALL — THE RAINBOW AT WAR, F. J. Heer Printing Co., Columbus, Ohio, 1936 / **168-169** From HISTORY OF THE FIRST DIVISION / **170-171** Col. E. D. Cooke; from AMERICANS VS. GERMANS, Infantry Journal Press / **172-173** John Dos Passos; from THREE SOLDIERS by John Dos Passos, © 1921; Houghton Mifflin / **176-177** Gen. William Mitchell; from MEMOIRS OF WORLD WAR I, Random House / **178-179** Hans Hanssen; from DIARY OF A DYING EMPIRE / **186-187** Gen. Sir Archibald Wavell; from ALLENBY, A STUDY IN GREATNESS, Oxford University Press / **188-189** Erich Maria Remarque; from ALL QUIET ON THE WESTERN FRONT, Little Brown, © by Erich Maria Remarque / **190-191** F. M. Cutlack, editor WAR LETTERS OF GENERAL SIR JOHN MONASH, Angus & Robertson Ltd., Sidney, 1931 / **190-191** Sir Phillip Gibbs; from THE WAY TO VICTORY, Doubleday, 1919 / **192-193** Horace L. Baker; from AR-

GONNE DAYS, Aberdeen Weekly, Aberdeen, Miss / **198-199**
William March; from COMPANY K, Peter Smith Co / **202-
203** Christian A. Bach, Henry Noble Hall, from THE
FOURTH DIVISION, issued by the Fourth Division, 1920 /
208-209 From The Memoirs of Marshal Foch / **210-211**
Same / **214-215**.

photo

8-9 Culver, Bettmann Archive / **10-11** Culver / **14-15** Bett-
mann Archive / **16-17** Bettmann Archive / **18-19** Pix / **10-21**
Bettmann Archive / **22-23** Culver, Bettmann Archive / **24-25**
Culver / **26-27** Ullstein / **28-29** Culver, Bettmann Archive /
30-31 Culver / **32-33** Imperial War Museum / **34-35** Bett-
mann Archive / **36-37** Bettmann Archive / **38-39** Bettmann
Archive / **42-43** European **44-45** Bettmann Archive / **46-47**
Bettmann Archive / **48-49** Culver / **50-51** Ullstein / **52-53**
Culver / **54-55** Culver / **56-57** Pix / **58-59** Culver / **60-61**
Pix / **62-63** Bettmann Archive / **64-65** Culver / **66-67** Bettmann Archive / **68-69** Bettmann Archive / **70-71** Bettmann
Archive / **72-73** European / **74-75** Bettmann Archive / **76-77**
Bettmann Archive / **80-81** Culver / **82-83** Bettmann Archive
/ **84-85** Bettmann Archive, Culver / **90-91** Bettmann Archive
/ **92-93** Ullstein, European /**94-95** Bettmann Archive, Ullstein / **96-97** Bettmann Archive / **98-99** Bettmann Archive /
100-101 Pix / **104-105** Pix / **106-107** Bettmann Archive /
108-109 Culver / **110-111** Bettmann Archive / **114-115** Culver / **122-123** European / **126-127** Pix / **128-129** Culver,
Bettmann Archive / **130-131** Ullstein / **132-133** Culver /
134-135 The National Archives / **138-139** European / **142-
143** Culver / **148-149** Bettmann Archive / **150-151** Culver /
152-153 Bettmann Archive / **154-155** Bettmann Archive,
Culver / **160-161** The National Archives / **162-163** Culver /
164-165 Culver / **166-167** Bettmann Archive / **168-169**
Culver / **172-173** Culver / **174-175** The National Archives /
176-177 Culver / **178-179** Bettmann Archive / **180-181** Culver / **182-183** The National Archives / **190-191** Culver/ **192-
193** Culver / **194-195** The National Archives / **196-197** The
National Archives / **198-199** Culver / **200-201** Pix / **202-203**
Culver / **204-205** The National Archives / **206-207** The National Archives, Bettmann Archives / **208-209** Bettmann
Archives / **212-213** The National Archives / Cover — The
National Archives, Pix, Culver, European, Tom Funderburk.